Drawing with Squiggles & Wiggles

Drawing with
Squiggles & Wiggles

Create 100+ Cartoons with Fun Shapes!

 **Get Creative 6**

DRAWING WITH Christopher Hart

An imprint of **Get Creative 6**
19 West 21st Street, Suite 601, New York, NY 10010
Sixthandspringbooks.com

Editor
LAURA COOKE

Creative Director
IRENE LEDWITH

Designer
JENNIFER MARKSON

Chief Executive Officer
CAROLINE KILMER

President
ART JOINNIDES

Chairman
JAY STEIN

Names: Hart, Christopher, 1957- author.
Title: Drawing with squiggles & wiggles : create 100+ cartoons with fun shapes! / Christopher Hart.
Other titles: Drawing with squiggles and wiggles
Description: New York, New York : Drawing with Christopher Hart, [2023] | Audience: Ages 5+
Identifiers: LCCN 2022041899 | ISBN 9781684620586 (set)
Subjects: LCSH: Cartoon characters in art--Juvenile literature. | Drawing--Technique--Juvenile literature. | BISAC: JUVENILE NONFICTION / Art / Cartooning | JUVENILE NONFICTION / Art / Techniques
Classification: LCC NC1764 .H363 2023 | DDC 741.5/1--dc23/eng/20220916
LC record available at https://lccn.loc.gov/2022041899

Manufactured in China

3 5 7 9 10 8 6 4 2

christopherhartbooks.com
facebook.com/CARTOONS.MANGA
youtube.com/user/chrishartbooks

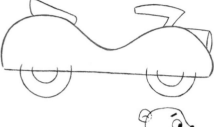

Dedicated to all future artists and cartoonists.

Contents

oink!

Intro to Drawing Fun

Everyone has scribbled a squiggle or a wiggle, but did you know that you can use them both to create funny animals, people, magical characters, and even thing-a-ma-bobs? When you create a drawing from a squiggle or a wiggle, you can't make a mistake! This book will show you how to turn those spontaneously drawn lines into real cartoons. There are tons of different squiggles and wiggles in this book that are the starting points for drawing people, places, pets, and so much more. Let's try them out together!

Animals Big & Small

You can use these ideas and techniques to create any type of animal, from a squirrel to an elephant. Exaggeration is also important. It looks funny if you can make your squiggle look even squigglier! In addition to serving as the basic shape of an animal, wiggles and squiggles can also be used as funny touches, such as the ears, trunk, or tail.

Cute Caterpillar

One easy way to create characters is to use a wiggly guideline to indicate the back. You'll see more of this fun approach throughout this book.

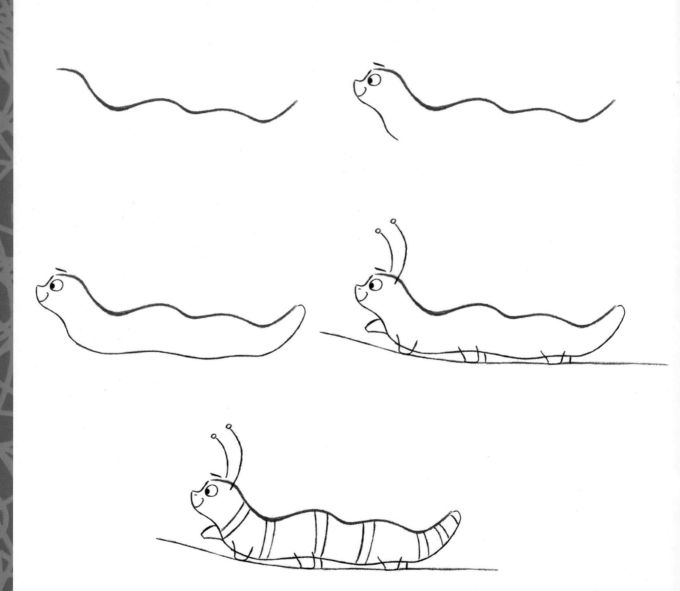

Alligator

By repeating squiggly lines in different places throughout a character, you create a stylish look. But don't get too close to its stylish teeth!

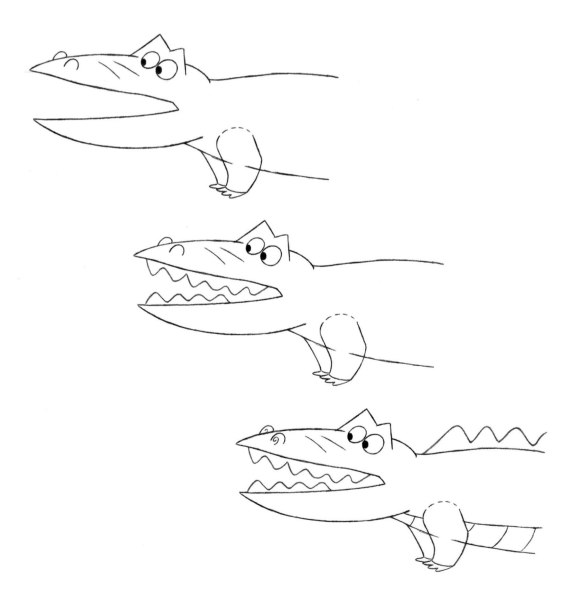

Bunny Wiggle

Some shapes can be left open because other things, like clothing or the foreground, will end up covering them. In this picture, the tall grass covers the bottom of the bunny, which can remain open.

Bad Bunny

It's practically a cartooning law that round and plump shapes make funny bad characters—they're too cute to be scary! Keep the head wide and the limbs short.

Baby Koala Needs a Hug

To create a baby animal, draw a big, round head and a small body.

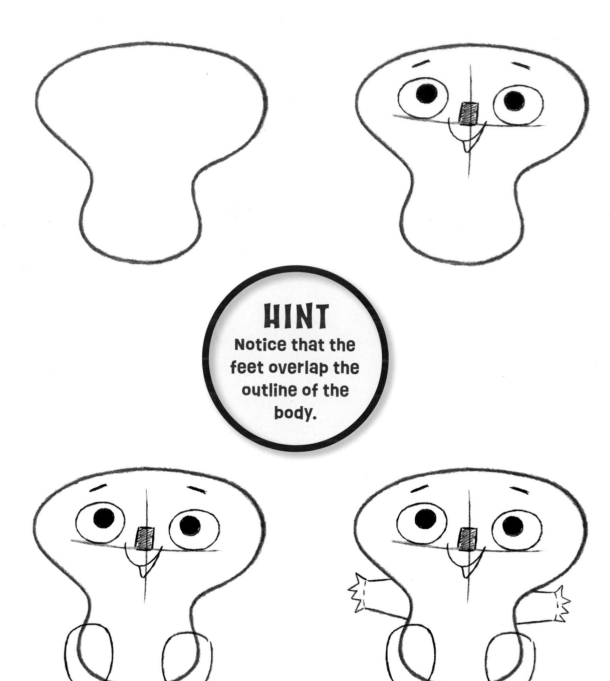

HINT
Notice that the feet overlap the outline of the body.

HUG! HUG !

Angry Sheep

Squiggly lines are used to create many popular cartoon character traits, from hairdos to sheep's wool. This sheep has cornered the market on squiggles. Don't ask him about his day.

Muskrat

The muskrat is based on a lightbulb shape, or Muskratus-lightbulbus. I had a relative whose head was this shape. Every time he went to the movies, people would ask him to turn his head off.

Squirrel Dilemma

Real squirrels have small heads and pudgy bodies. But cartoon animals are based on big heads and small bodies. So, we'll exaggerate the squirrel's eyes and tail, and that will make it work!

More Squirrels!

This little guy is drawn with two sets of swerving lines: one for the tail and another for the back. Notice that the character is leaning to the right.

HINT
Notice that the tail is longer than the body.

Fox

The fox's snout is skinnier than the snouts of dogs or wolves. For a finishing touch, draw fluffy cheeks behind the ears. Pair up the pointed ears.

HINT
A gentle slope of the snout gives the character a charming look.

Opossum

I always have trouble spelling the word opossum, so I developed a technique to get it right, which is, I look it up in the dictionary. (I might do it with other words, too.) The opossum looks like a mouse but with a longer and narrower snout.

HINT
Draw the back as a tall bump.

Bull

Oversized spiral nostrils add humor to the cartoon bull. The spirals spin in the same direction, which in this case is to the left. If they were to spin in opposite directions, they would probably make him sneeze.

Cow

This is the classic wiggly-woggly shape, which is used for cartoon cows. Notice that the top of the head is small (the wiggly) and the nose part below is large (the woggly). A cup-shaped chin finishes the overall outline.

Horse

By drawing squiggles on only one side of the mane, you create a funny look without making it appear too busy.

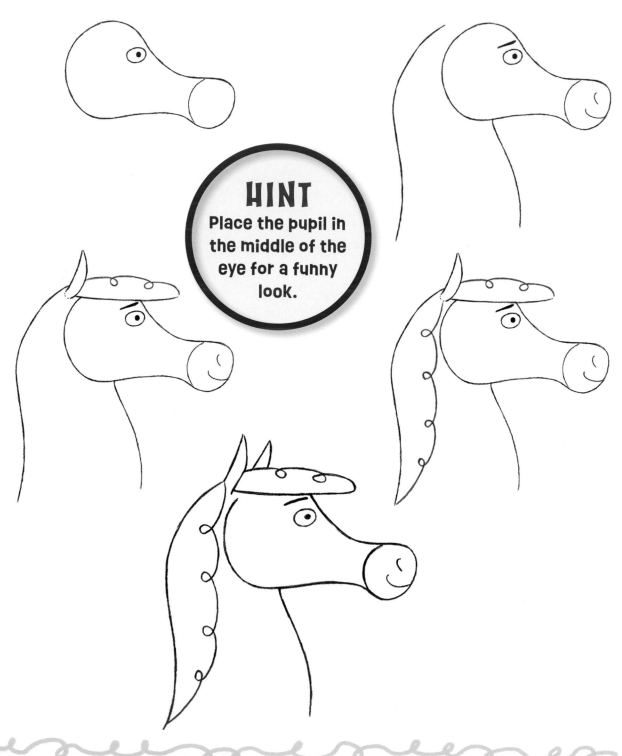

HINT
Place the pupil in the middle of the eye for a funny look.

Ram's Horns

Sometimes nature creates its own designs,
like the corkscrew-style horns of the ram,
which make it look strong. Draw a thick neck
in order to support those heavy horns.

HINT
The back of
the neck is a
straight line.

Pony

Ponies are charming animals that want to be your friend. Even if you don't want to be their friend, they still want to be your friend so bad. I don't know how to get away from a pony. Right now, I am typing this next to a pony.

HINT

Note how ponies are built:
- The pudgy body is in the shape of a jelly bean.
- The legs are short.
- The front of the head is flat.

Miniature Unicorn

The head shape of a unicorn is called a "preposterous oval." The head is super-wide with a small bump-out for the mouth. Place the base of the horn between the two eyebrows. But be careful—it's sharp.

Camel

The prize for the wiggliest of lines must go to the camel and its hump. The line of the back is a series of uneven bumps. They're a funny, odd type of animal, sort of like a cross between a deer and a ski slope.

HINT
The camel's neck dips in the middle.

The front leg bends in three places.

Scooter Scramble

Here's just one more reason why bear cubs shouldn't try to ride scooters. The scooter is drawn with a long wavy line on top and a straight line under it. It's funnier if you draw the bear cub reaching for the handlebars. He looks more helpless that way.

HINT
The puff of smoke is also a squiggle.

Cheerful Bug

Nothing seems to bug this guy. I must apologize to you and to future generations for that terrible pun. I was just winging it. I apologize for that, too.

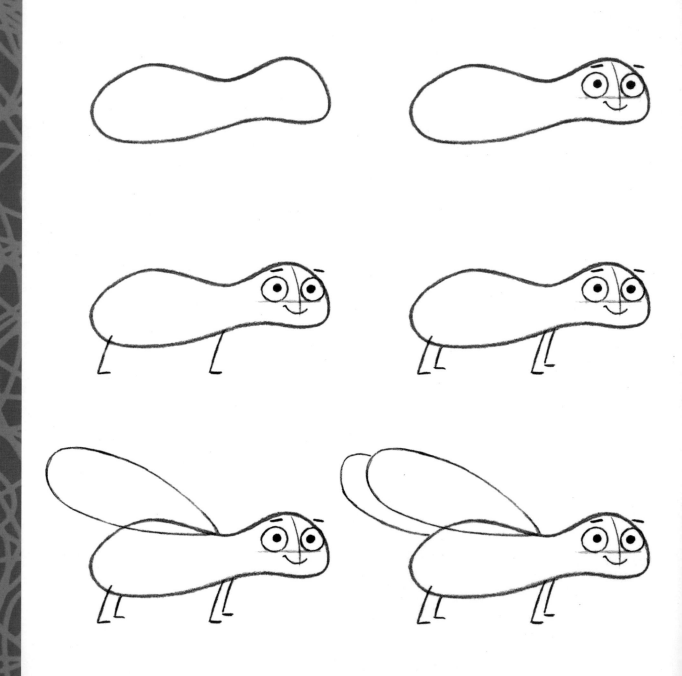

Bumpy Bug

The most interesting design element of this character is the overall shape: The back is created with three overlapping bumps, while the underside is a straight line.

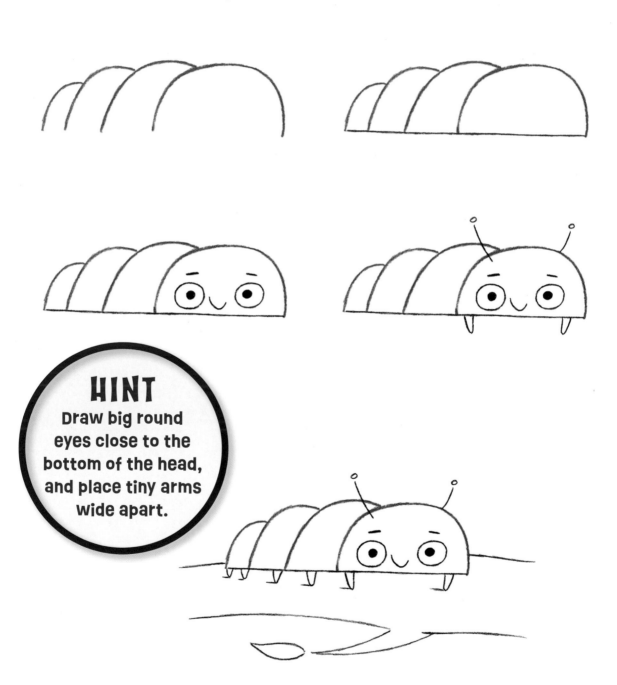

HINT
Draw big round eyes close to the bottom of the head, and place tiny arms wide apart.

Oinky 1 & Oinky 2

Pigs have a special quality that few other animals possess. It's derived from their unique snouts. They're coiled up in the most conspicuous way in the middle of the face.

Insomnia

Don't worry, big guy, only three more months until spring. I wonder if his cave gets Wi-Fi.

HINT
Draw a series of bumps descending from high to low.

Goofy Buck

The squiggles of the antlers are funny, but they should also look powerful. Therefore draw the antlers thickest at the top.

HINT
• The antlers are rounded at the ends.
• The head tilts slightly down.

Squiggly Trunk

Elephants are so thick and immobile that cartoonists look for ways to add dynamic visuals to the character. Turning the trunk into a design element does the trick!

HINT
Draw a dip in the middle of the trunk.

Bear Chef

Sometimes, a double-shape can be used as an accessory to a character, like this chef's hat. The hands mimic "people" gestures to humanize the character.

HINT
The hat and head are roughly the same size.

Duck

A swirling line defines the duck's body, then continues to spiral inward and becomes the wing.

HINT
- The chest pushes forward.
- Draw the legs toward the back of the body.

Cold Canary

Her mother kept reminding her to fly south for the winter, but did she listen? Draw this little, confused bird with a puzzled expression. Draw big eyes, aimed skyward. Lift the eyebrows so that they're diagonal.

Silly Sssssnake

I like to draw goofy snakes so as to make them appear harmless. One way to do this is to coil them in a funny way. The second is to hide the chin so it's not visible.

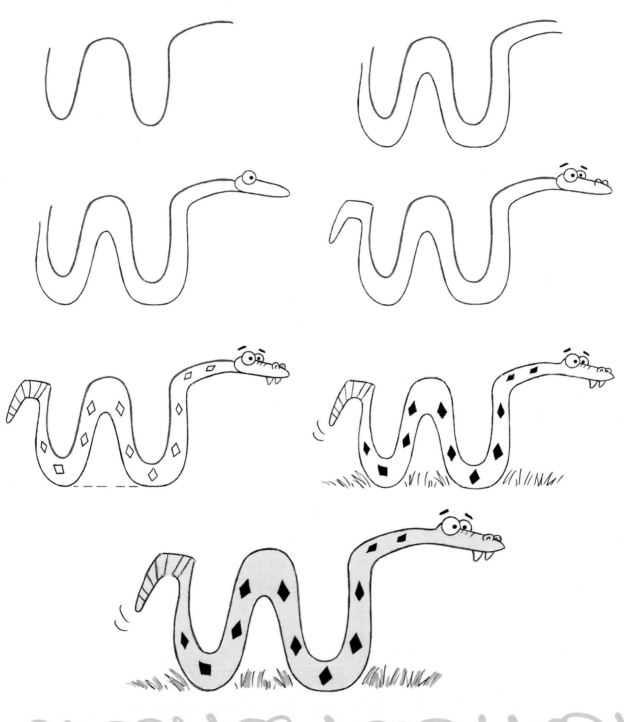

Dinosaur in a Hurry!

Big characters begin with funny shapes. Their heads are small compared to their giant bodies, and this is true whether they're humans or dinosaurs.

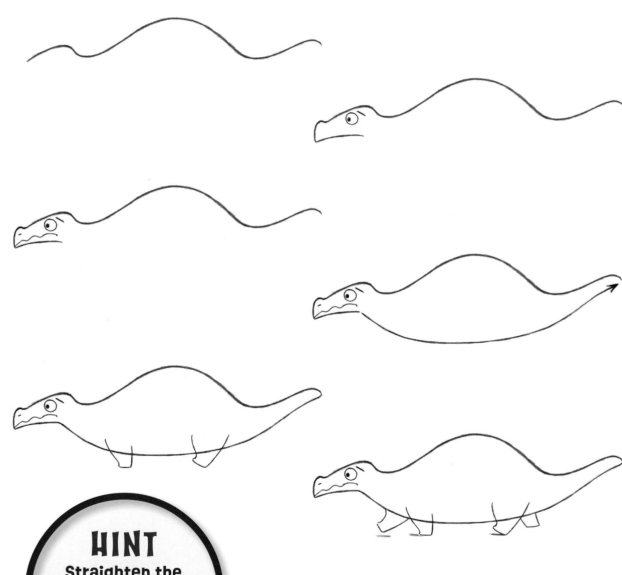

HINT
Straighten the legs, which creates a funny run for big characters.

Harmless Lion

As cartoonists, we often are called upon to turn wild animals into friendly looking animals. Here are a few ways you can do it:

- Draw a round, oversized head.

- Add eyelashes to the eyes.

- Draw the pose like a dog's or a cat's pose. (See the next chapter!)

WATER ADVENTURES!

The water is the ultimate playground for cartoon characters. Some dogs like to surf, and some fish like to fetch. In an ocean scene, you can find a little humor everywhere.

Surfing Dog

This drawing is all about overlap: The wave overlaps the surfboard, and the surfboard overlaps the dog.

Octo-Bumps

The key to this layout is drawing the octo-bumps wide on top and wide on the bottom. The sand line, which is drawn under the creature, is a series of smaller bumps.

Deep Water

To portray deep water, draw multiple lines of waves across the picture. Make sure the tip of each wave doesn't line up directly with the tip of the wave above it, but to the side instead.

Electric Eel

It must be hard to sneak up on another fish when you're constantly glowing. To portray electricity, cartoonists like to use jagged lightning effects. The eel itself is drawn like a flat snake with a long ridge down its back.

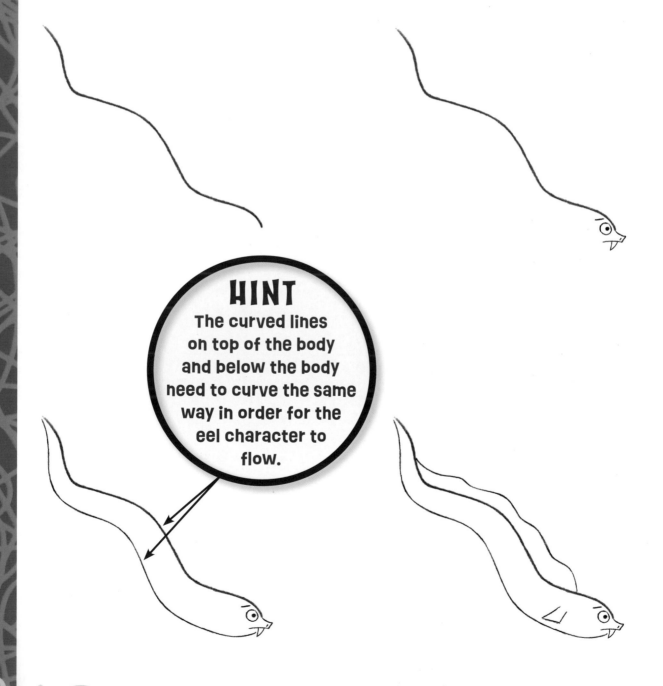

HINT
The curved lines on top of the body and below the body need to curve the same way in order for the eel character to flow.

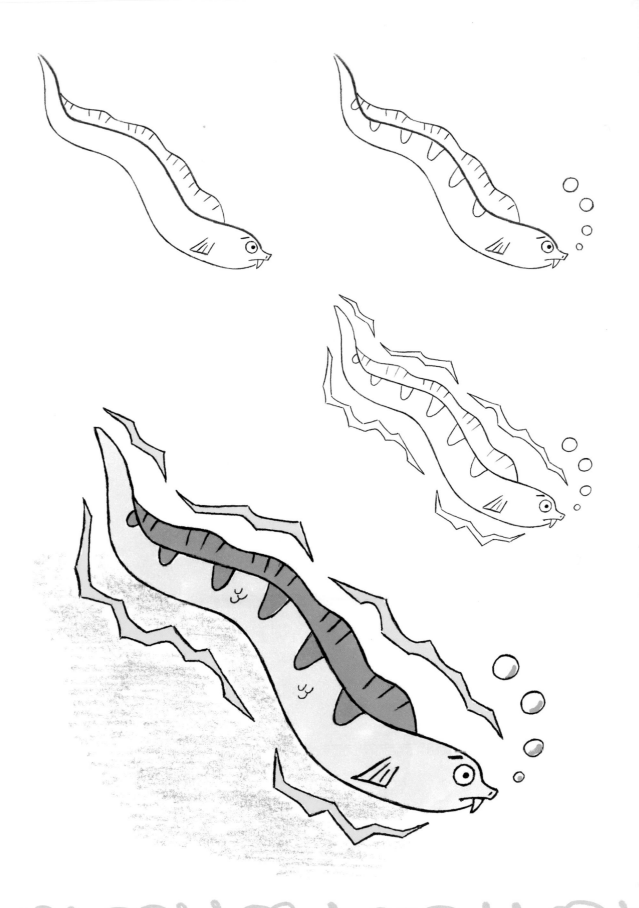

Friendly Shark

The surface of the water is choppy, whereas the line of the seabed is calm. Next, we turn to the shark. How do you draw a friendly shark with sharp teeth and a dorsal fin on its back? Easy! Just draw them tiny.

Speedboat

Most bears don't get to do this. They need to find a cartoonist to help them. Waves create a strong design on a page. The scalloped look creates the illusion that the boat is moving fast through the water.

HINT
Keep the tips of the waves the same height.

Dogs & Cats

We've already seen squiggles and wiggles used to draw almost every kind of animal, but dogs and cats deserve a chapter of their own. Curling tails, drooping ears, and fluffs of fur—they're all made up of natural, looping lines that make it easy to turn a squiggle or wiggle into a precious pet. Let's learn how to do it!

DOGS
Funny Puppy

Start by drawing a line with a giant dip in the middle. The shape in the center becomes the head, and the shapes at the ends become the ears.

Cuddly Puppy

This shape is similar to a salt shaker that didn't pass the quality inspection test. But it works for our purposes. Notice that the head is squashed on top of the body. That gives it a puppyish look.

Where Did I Bury My Bone?!

The technical name for this red, squiggly line is the "almost circle." Instead of connecting where it began, it continues to swirl around.

Horseshoe Shapes

This pooch is based on two overlapping horseshoes: One is up, and the other is upside down. The top horseshoe is a little wider than the bottom horseshoe.

HINT
Leave space where the horseshoes overlap, which will create the mouth area.

Astonished Pup!

A super-squiggly shape can create all types of energetic mouth expressions.

Yum, Yum, Yum!

This shape combines the head and body into one form. It's known as the "curious oval." No one is certain how it got its name, but it's on file at the main office at the Guild of Wiggles & Squiggles.

Doodle Dog

The Doodle Dog is a festival of squiggles. There are squiggles on the ears, squiggles on the head, and squiggles on the tail! There's even a ball of squiggles on the tip of the tail.

Alert Hound

This looping line starts at the head, then travels to the feet and curls around the thigh. This creates a pleasing flow to the pose.

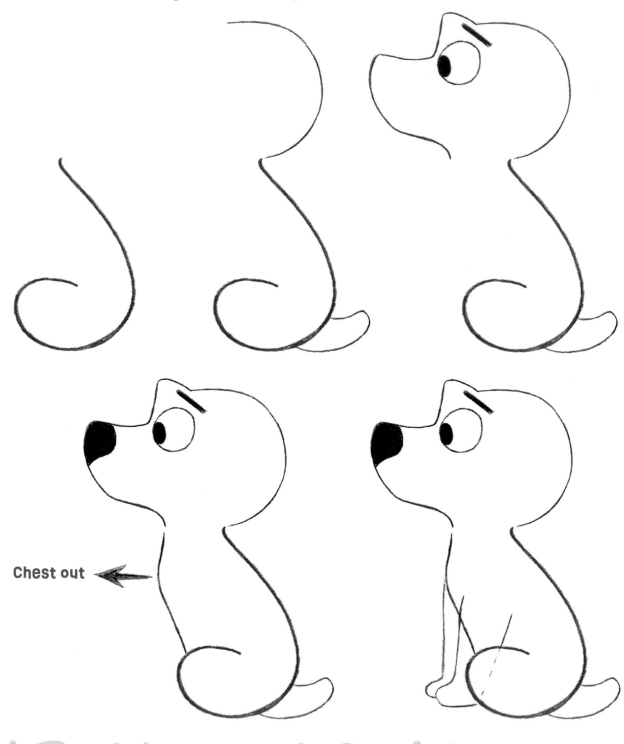

Chest out

HINT

Here's two helpful tips to note:
• The back of the head protrudes behind the ear.
• The chest pops out just a bit, even on puppies.

Dog in a Long Pose

When a dog sits tummy-side down, its back dips in the middle, revealing curves and bumps, which are created by the shoulders and hips.

Dog Hobbies

Most dogs like to play tug-of-war with a sock, but cartoon dogs have even more hobbies to choose from. Notice the floppy ears, which create a sense of motion. This is also a good example of a symmetrical pose.

CATS
Fluffiness!

Even if the face looks like a ball of fur, it still needs a wiggly foundation shape to get started.

HINT
Leave the fur open on the sides of the face.

Kitty

Draw the arms inside the outline of the body but the whiskers outside of the body.

Cat Sat

The line of the back travels down to the tail and curls underneath the body so you can't even see its foot!

Cat Standing

The shape of the body is a dented oval. Or, to be technical about it, a "doval." The legs taper to the feet. Finally, a cat's head is relatively small compared to its body.

Broken-Hearted Kitten

Being able to capture a "dear" look on a young character is essential for cartoonists. The main elements that go into this expression are:

- Sloping eyebrows
- A tiny lower lip
- Delicate little paws

Curly-Tailed Kitty

By curling the tip of the tail, you add interest to the pose. This is especially useful when drawing stationary poses.

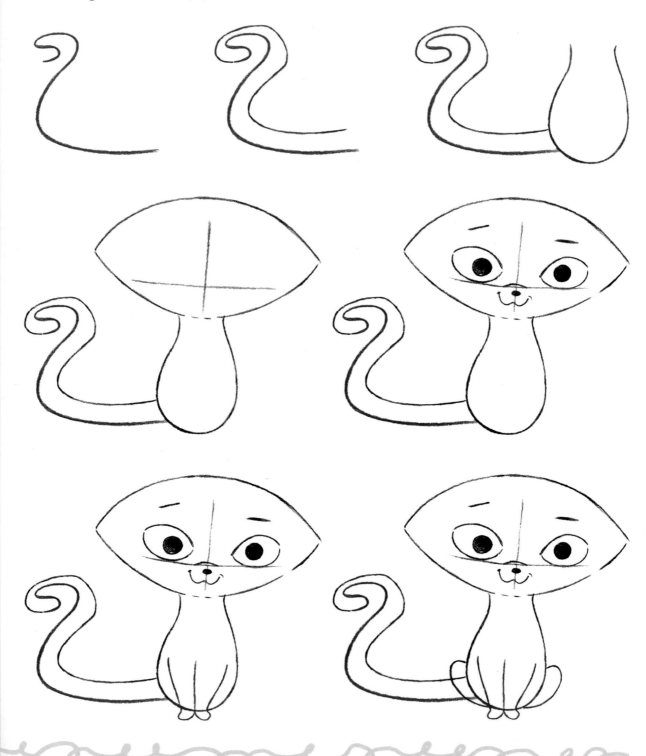

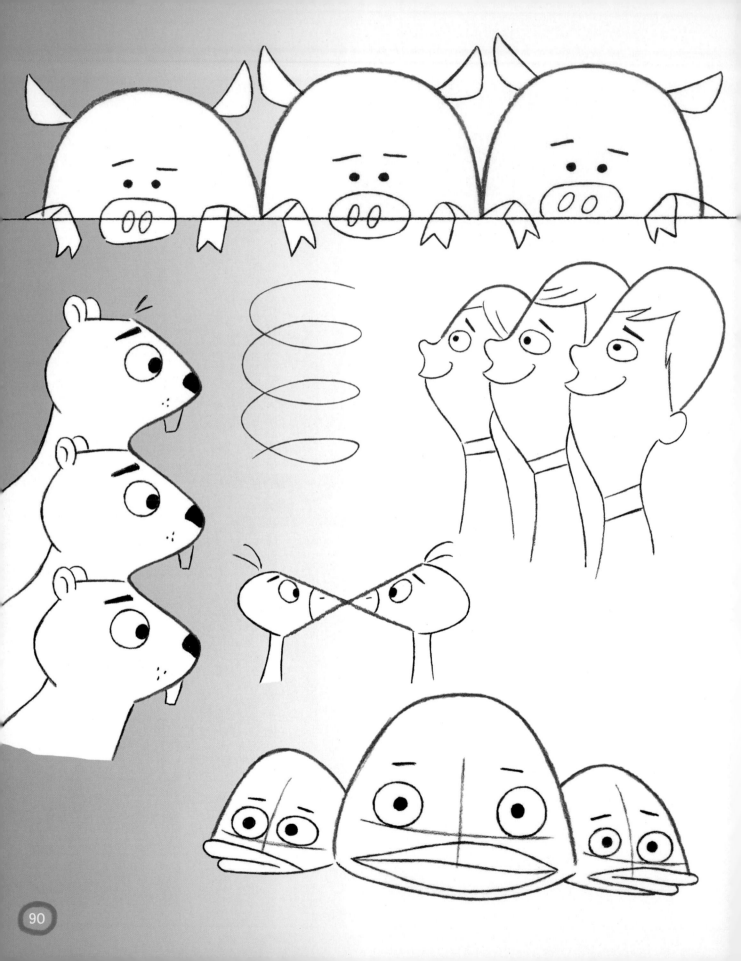

Drawing Tricks

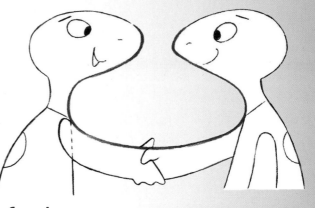

These drawing tricks are fun! And they're based on a simple principle called *symmetry*. That means the characters in each scene are practically identical, even if they face

in different directions. It doesn't need to be perfect. Just have fun with it!

Dog Twins

Start off with a single line that has two big bumps. Draw a straight line across the bottom of the bumps. By adding details, step-by-step, you'll see the dog twins emerge—like magic!

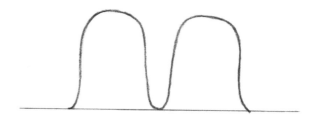

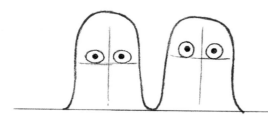

Best Friends

What, at first, looks like nothing more than a zigzaggy line quickly turns into a pair of wolves who happen to be best friends.

HINT
The noses point the way for the direction of the faces.

Nervous Dogs

Which is the brave one? Neither! But together they can face any danger. These puppies are based on a line in the shape of the letter S.

HINT
Both dogs glance to the left.

Prairie Dogs

Here's another fun pair of characters we can create from an S line. Prairie dogs have expressive faces because their eyes are so big.

HINT
Keep the mouth small but the tooth big.

A Row of Bears

To make this trick work, draw each curve the same as the one above it or below it. Draw the nose and mouth close to the bottom of the face on each head.

Turtle Greeting

If you've ever wanted to see the secret greeting turtles use to say hello to each other, here it is. It's the official handshake of the Fraternal Order of Reptiles with Shells, or the F.O.R.S., for short.

HINT
Position the characters so they're not too close together and have to reach out to make contact.

Beak to Beak

This is a simple design: All you need is to draw the back of the head on the left side of the X and the back of the head on the right side of the X, and you'll have created the framework for the two characters.

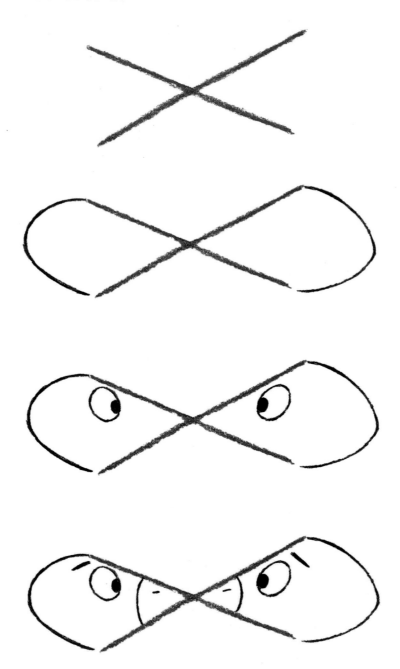

More Bird Tricks!

The trick for this drawing is to make the two heads, which are facing left, very round, as shown by the red line in step one. That sets up the framework for the single head facing in the opposite direction (right).

HINT
Draw the eyes close to the top of the head.

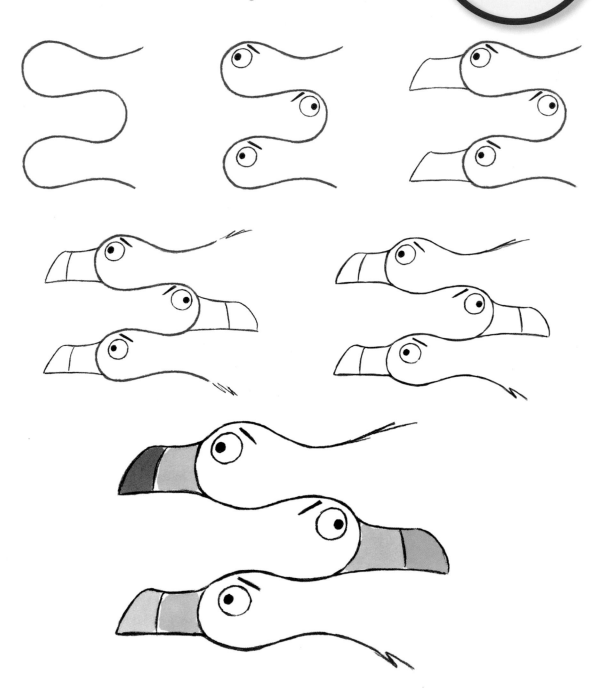

Curious Piglets

These little fellows are based on three continuous piggy bumps. In cartooning, repetition is often used to create humor, and here, it seems to work!

HINT
Draw their snouts hanging over the fence.

oink!

Alert Squirrels

There must be a sale on acorns today. Notice something interesting about this picture: The heads are stacked on top of one another, but the bodies are drawn at an angle. That makes the bodies clearer to see.

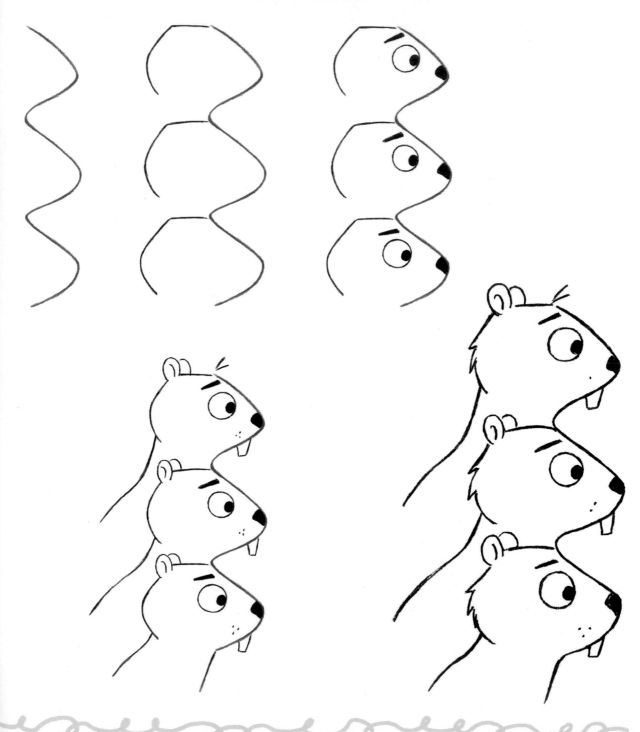

At the Movies

This amusing scene is created with simple overlapping bumps. The foreheads of the characters are drawn at an angle, to make it appear as if they are looking up at the screen.

HINT
Leave a little space between the bodies.

Three Monkeys!

These monkeys refused to stand still for the drawing, so I had to bribe them with a banana. Did they say thank you? No. I try not to hold a grudge against my cartoon characters but it's not always easy.

Fish Taking a Break

When you place one character ahead of the others, try increasing its size as well. This will create an interesting visual dynamic.

Bird Brothers

Everyone's heard the saying, "Birds of a feather flock together." But have you heard, "Draw two birds next to each other because it's funny"? There's a reason you haven't heard of it. I just made it up, which doesn't make it any less true!

HINT
In the final drawing, add a line for the back of the taller bird brother.

People

In this section, we'll have fun creating different people and personalities. Squiggles and wiggles are perfect for this. They can be used as the basis for drawing the cartoon head, hair, and expression. Cartoonists like to draw the overall shape of a character before working on the details. We'll start the same way.

Wavy Hair

Hairstyles use a lot of squiggles and wiggles. But we need to put them onto something, so we'll first draw the basic head shapes.

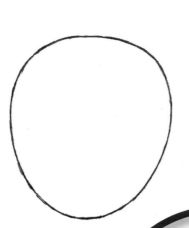
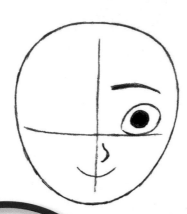

HINT
The hairstyle will cover the character's right eye, therefore, we can leave it out of the step-by-step drawings.

Hair Squiggles

This is a famous technique for drawing cartoon hair, and it's been used on many funny characters. The trick is to make the little squiggly parts the same size and shape.

HINT
- Keep the squiggly parts open.
- The back of the head is drawn with a straight line.

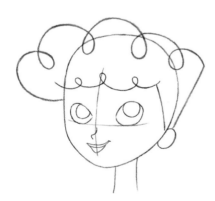

Glamorous

This character is drawn with so many squiggles that they make the head look twice as big as it really is.

HINT
The left side of the hair is bigger.

Super-Wavy

The hair travels from the top right of the head to the bottom left of the face, with a pit stop for a wiggle in the middle. The end of the hair is drawn with a straight line, which gives it a sharp and stylish look.

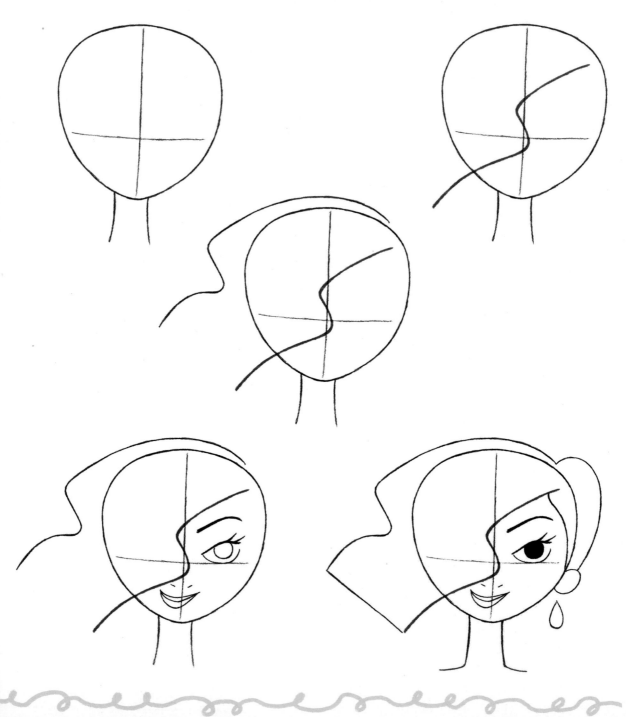

Looping Line

This beach lover's hair blows in the summer breeze. As it goes back, it flips up. Drawing the eyebrows inside of the bangs is a popular technique among animators. It allows them to emphasize an expression that might otherwise be hidden.

Hair Wiggly-Squiggly

When the hairstyle is very wiggly and very squiggly, you can leave the bottom open. That gives it a funny, lively look.

Teen Hair

Hair can be closely cropped but still look wavy. For a cartoony look, extend the hair way past the forehead.

HINT
Only the top line needs to wiggle. The rest can be straight.

Mustache Man

Start with two overlapping horseshoes. The top line will become the mustache and the bottom line will become the chin.

Strong Guy

By drawing two wavy lines next to each other,
you create an athletic character type.

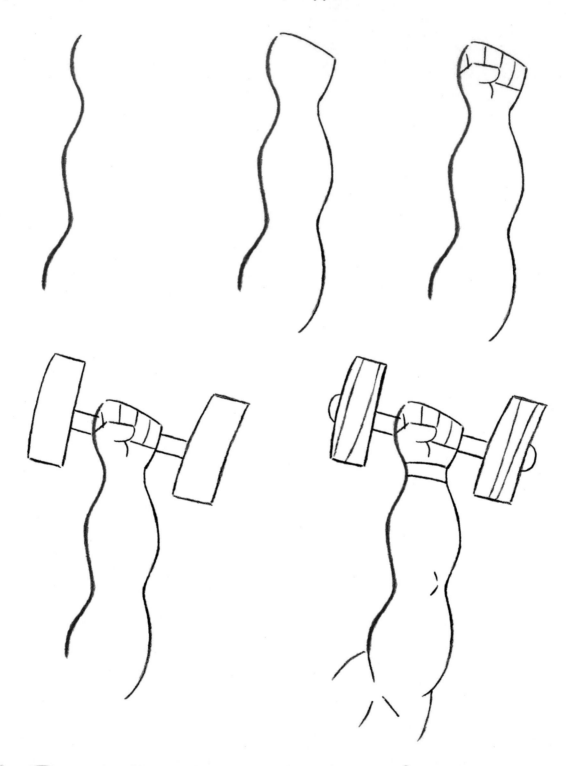

Princess Hair

Princess hair is the same as peasant hair, except when it's princess hair, you own the castle in the background. When drawing long princess hair, fluff it out at the sides to give it more body.

HINT
Draw lines for bangs and leave them open for a natural look.

Three Shapes

Begin with three disconnected shapes. Then, step-by-step, add lines and details to bring the character together and create a finished cartoon.

Profile

In a profile, the hair covers much of the face, including the ear. To make it look natural, draw it bumpy and wavy.

Giant Ponytail

This ponytail is longer than the girl! That's one example of how proportions can be used to create humor.

HINT
When a character is miniaturized, reduce the amount of detail in the picture.

Surprised Hair

Hair can be used to show a big reaction and to get some laughs. It's like having an exclamation point over your head, except it needs to be trimmed every few months. Taper the hair all the way to the back.

HINT
Draw the top of the hair with a wiggly but horizontal line.

So Stylish

This hairdo is deceptive in that it looks challenging but is actually easy to draw! Here's how you do it: Break up the haircut so that it's based on three simple lines—left side, top side, and right side.

Girl Based on a Figure Eight

This character starts out as a figure eight that is left open at the bottom. Next, draw a straight line across the bottom, which creates the jacket. Make the hood thick so it looks snug.

HINT
Draw a line to create the bottom of the jacket

Drawing the Body

Because the body has many moving parts, cartoonists begin by simplifying it. The best way to do that is to create a basic outline.

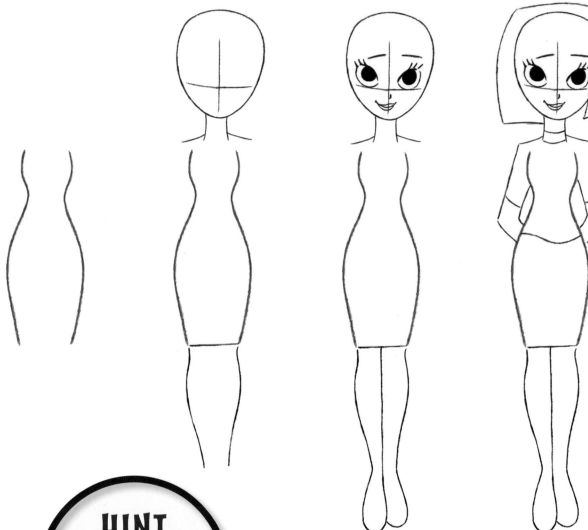

HINT
The waist, hips, and legs are curvy, with no straight lines.

Joyful Teacher

One of her students remembered what the word *plethora* meant! It's a minor victory. Excitable characters are often drawn with their arms and legs in motion.

Executive Mom

Once again, we're having fun with proportions in order to bring humor and energy to the character.

Cute Monsters & More Funny Stuff

I had almost finished drawing this book when I received an urgent call from a monster. He and his fellow monsters complained that they had been left out of the book. Something had to be done! With smoke flying off of my pencil, I got busily to work. I must say, I received the nicest monster thank you note. Enjoy!

Blob Thing

Blobs are shapes with only a hint of arms and legs. They make great monsters. But they have a curious resemblance to a floating glob of pudding.

HINT
Draw the eyes close to the top of the head.

Space Bumps

Here's a trick for creating funny characters from simple shapes. Draw them so they're pretty much identical, but give them completely different expressions.

Puzzled Monster

The squiggly mouth is so expressive that it can steal the show from those kooky monster eyes. Notice how far back into the head the mouth travels. It's almost as far back as the ears. If it had ears.

HINT
Draw the mouth like a wave.

Glob of Goo

This monster is based on a random shape. But is it really random? If you look closely, you'll see that its left side is about the same as its right side!

Monster Jr. and Dad

What can you do to infuse personality into a rectangle? Add a bend in the back. That will cause the tummy to push forward, which creates an endearing look. The oversized eyes are also a cute touch.

Peary Scary!

Animators have a term for this technique: *human personification*. Or you can use my term, which I believe works just as well: *pear with a face.* When you draw the mouth in the middle of the face, it will make the pear look as if it has a big chin, which is funny!

Bad Dragon!

This character starts out as a circle that forgot where it's supposed to stop. Notice that the snout is short—that's typical on young characters, even made-up ones like a dragon.

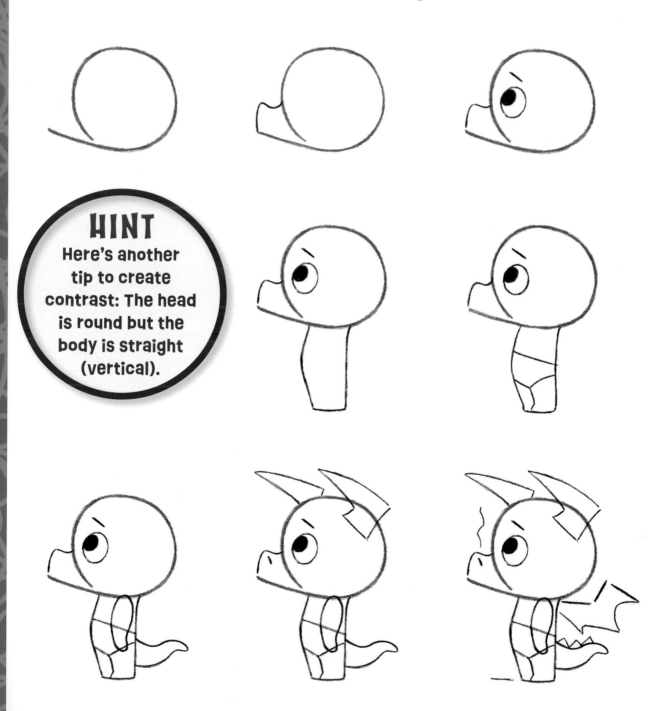

HINT
Here's another tip to create contrast: The head is round but the body is straight (vertical).

Monster Colors

How do we draw a monster, or any character, to make it look scared? Start by drawing tiny pupils in the center of the eyes. Then draw the mouth wide open. Excuse me a second, I'm going to have to calm him down.

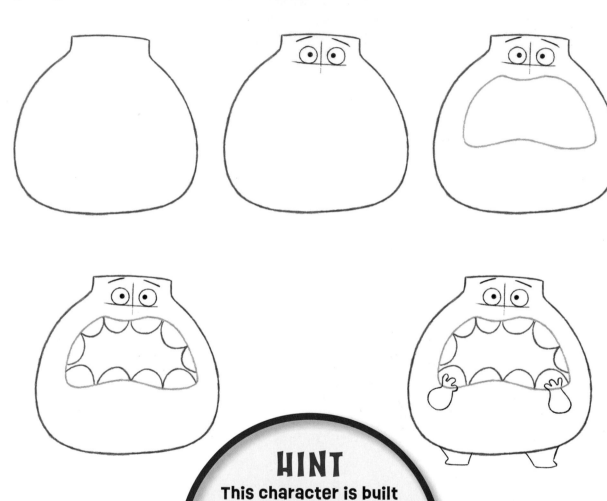

HINT
This character is built on three types of shapes, as indicated by the different colors:
- Red (outline)
- Powder blue (mouth)
- Navy blue (teeth)

Grumpy Alien

This irritable little life form is based on a wiggly body and a wiggly tail. When you have only one eye to draw, you have to give it a bigger expression, because you have less to work with—but the effect is funny.

Alien Baby

Baby characters, whether they're animals, humans, or from neighboring galaxies, are based on simple shapes. This little fella also has squid-like tentacles that help him slither around (shown by the red line).

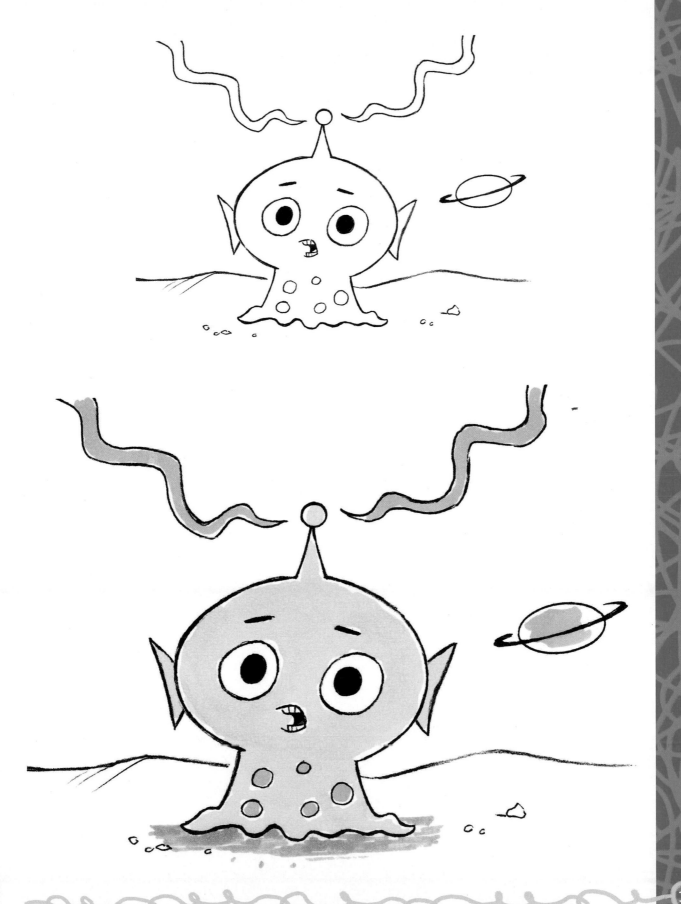

Repeated Shapes

Sometimes, monsters take the form of fast moving bands of characters, invading other planets. Placement is key when you draw multiple characters.

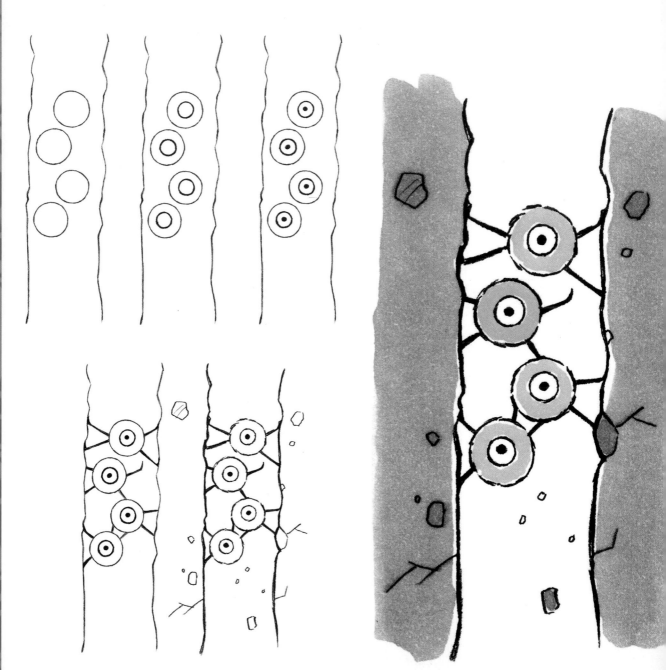

Magical Wand

Wands are great. You can draw them with your characters to make them appear all powerful. When I was a kid, I tried to use one to make my parents obey my every command. They returned the wand.

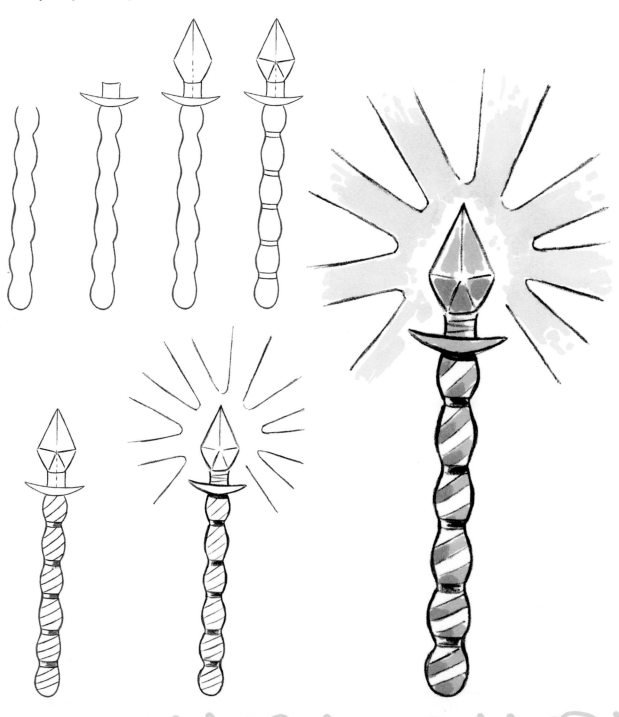

Elf

The visual theme, when drawing an elf or a fairy, is pointedness. The eyes are pointed, the nose is pointed, and the ears are pointed. But what about the basic overall outline? Yes! It begins with the tip of the hat!

Noodles—Yum, Yum, Yum!

Here's an example of taking an ordinary thing, like a noodle, and turning it into a dynamic element by zigzagging a line back and forth.

Ice Cream Delight

As a kid, I always wanted to draw an ice cream cone. I would buy some ice cream from the store, bring it home, get ready to draw it, and then something would happen and it would be gone. My parents would be like, what happened to your ice cream? I know, weird, right?

HINT
Those simple faces off to the side add to the feeling of anticipation.

HINT
When you have an easily recognizable image, like an ice cream cone, you don't need excess detail—the viewer will quickly be able to figure out what it is.

Bowling

The squiggly line is called a *motion line*. It shows that something is moving. When it's drawn with squiggles, it looks like it's bouncing too.

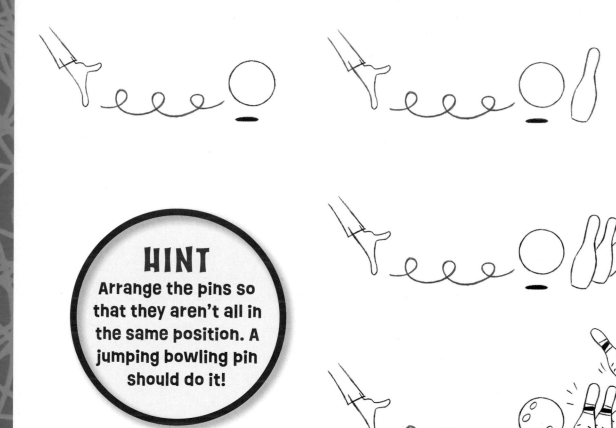

HINT

Arrange the pins so that they aren't all in the same position. A jumping bowling pin should do it!

Shell

Conch shells have a sort of crown on top, which is finished with a spike. The tricky part, if there is one, is the opening, which is shown in red. But we can simplify that, too.

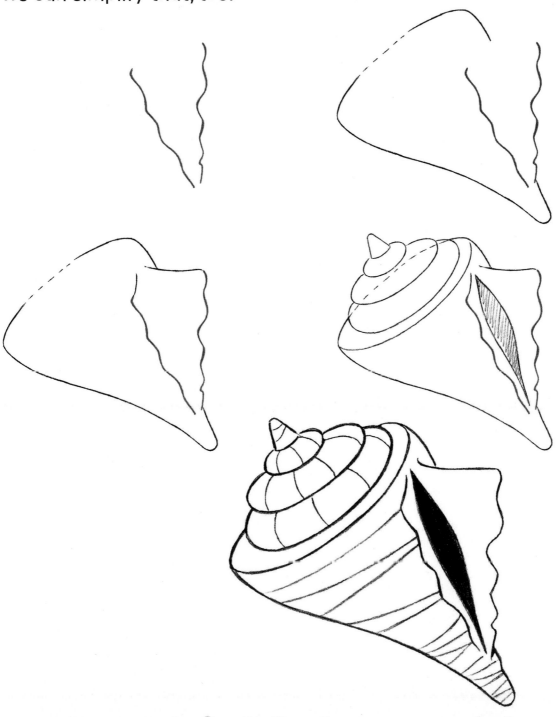

Clouds with Personalities

Here's another example of turning an inanimate object into a character—or in this case, several characters. The key is to give them personality. And we can use weather effects to make that happen.

Cloud template

Generic cloud face

Rain cloud

Lightning cloud

Hail cloud

Snow cloud

Cloud family

Eggs & Bacon

There are three things to be observed about this picture: Eggs are wiggly. Bacon is squiggly. And they're also kind of giggly! Notice that the squiggly lines in the bacon strips are identical. Scientists call this squiggularity.

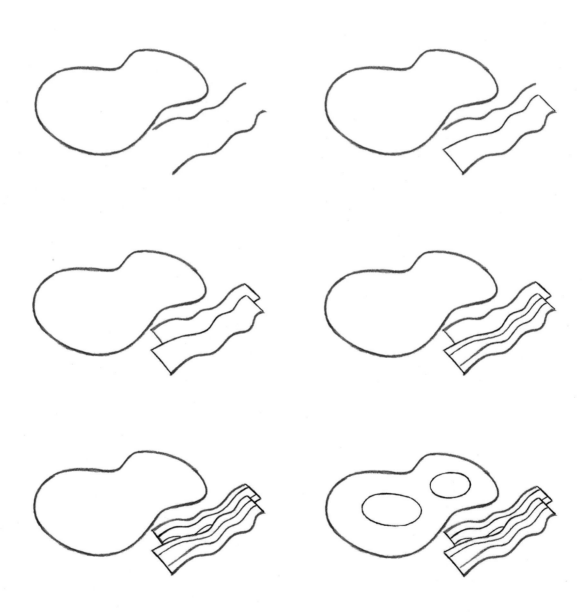

HINT
Draw the two eggs at uneven sizes, which makes it more interesting than if they're identical.

Worried Pie

People often think of a wedge of pie as a triangle, but it's actually a triangle in 3D. The most important part is the decoration on the top: the bumpy crown. It's the pastry version of a tiara made of dough. Poor little wedge of pie. Everyone likes it—too much!

Cypress Trees (with Apologies to Van Gogh!)

Tall trees based on squiggles and wiggles start off wide at ground level and rise up to a point. The horizon line (the ground) is drawn at the bottom of the picture, which makes the trees look even taller.

HINT

• Repeating the tree several times gives the image a sturdy look.
• Overlapping the hills makes the houses appear further into the distance.

Index